Out and About at the Fire Station

Field Trips

Written by Muriel L. Dubois • Illustrated by Anne McMullen

Content Advisor: Captain Mark Klose, B.S., NREMT-R
Director of Education and Safety, Bedford, New Hampshire, Safety Complex

Reading Advisor: Lauren A. Liang, M.A.
Literacy Education, University of Minnesota, Minneapolis, Minnesota

PICTURE WINDOW BOOKS
Minneapolis, Minnesota

In memory of my firefighter uncle, George Gagnon (1925–1992)—M.L.D.

This book was based on field trips hosted by firefighters at the Manchester, New Hampshire, Central Fire Station and the Bedford, New Hampshire, Safety Complex. Special thanks to Fire Chief Ed O'Reilly; firefighters Mark Lemay, John Briggs, and Rick Clement (of Manchester); and Captain Kevin Murray and Captain Mark Klose (of Bedford).

Designer: Melissa Voda
Page production: Picture Window Books
The illustrations in this book were rendered using watercolor and ink.

Picture Window Books
5115 Excelsior Boulevard
Suite 232
Minneapolis, MN 55416
1-877-845-8392
www.picturewindowbooks.com

Printed in the United States of America.
1 2 3 4 5 6 08 07 06 05 04 03

Library of Congress Cataloging-in-Publication Data
Dubois, Muriel L.
  Out and about at the fire station / written by Muriel L. Dubois ; illustrated by Anne McMullen.
    p. cm.
  Summary: Children visit a fire station and learn how firefighters do their work.
  ISBN 1-4048-0039-5 (Library binding : alk. paper)
  1. Fire extinction—Juvenile literature. 2. Fire stations—Juvenile literature. [1. Fire extinction.
2. Fire departments.] I. Title: At the fire station. II. McMullen, Anne, ill. III. Title.
  TH9148 .D83 2003
  628.9'2—dc21

2002006284

We're going on a field trip to the fire station. We can't wait!

Things to find out:
How do firefighters find fires?
What other jobs do firefighters have besides fighting fires?
Do firefighters sleep in their gear?
What do they do while they're waiting for fires?

Welcome to Main Street Fire Station. I'm Firefighter
Tim, and this is my partner, Firefighter Raj. This is our
garage and equipment room. We have an ambulance,
a ladder truck, a fire engine, and a rescue boat.

We use our ladder truck to rescue people who can't get
down the stairs. Firefighters also use ladders to reach the
top of a burning building. Inside the truck, we have

6   axes, hooks, and other firefighting tools.

The ladder on this truck can reach about 10 stories up. If a building is taller than that, firefighters must use the stairs inside the building to reach someone.

The chief's car carries special equipment. If the smoke is very thick, we use a special camera that helps us find people trapped in the smoke.

When there's a fire, people call 911 for help. A dispatcher gets the phone call and tells the firefighters where the fire is.

9

When we get to the fire, we connect the pumper truck to a fire hydrant to get water. Then the water comes out of the truck through a large hose like this one. The hoses are very heavy. It takes at least two firefighters to hold and point a hose.

Tanker trucks are used in places where there are no fire hydrants.
Some tankers hold 3,000 gallons (11,360 liters) of water.

Firefighters wear special clothes called turnout gear. We always leave our gear nearby, ready to wear. Our pants are already tucked into our boots so we can just jump into the boots and pull up the suspenders. Next we put on our coats. When we get to the fire, we pull on our hoods, helmets, gloves, face masks, and air tanks. Every inch of our skin is covered.

Turnout coats have three layers. The outer layer is made so it won't burn easily. The inner layers let body heat out but don't let smoky air reach the skin.

Fighting fires is not our only job. We're trained to help people who are sick or hurt. We do water rescues and clean up dangerous chemicals. For these jobs we wear special suits.

When firefighters clean up dangerous chemicals, it is called HAZMAT duty. HAZMAT means <u>haz</u>ardous <u>mat</u>erial.

15

Firefighters who work together at one station are called a company. The firefighters in a company practice teamwork. We cook together, eat together, and learn together. We even exercise and play games together to stay in shape.

Every firefighter works with a partner.
Partners watch out for each other.
Firefighters never go into a fire without their partners.

After the fire is out, we find out how the fire started. Some people start fires on purpose. This is a crime called arson. We use special dogs to find clues that help us solve arson crimes. Firefighter Gail is working with Ash-lee, our company's arson dog.

The best arson dogs are Labrador retrievers, because of their great sense of smell.

19

One fun way that firefighters practice their skills is by competing in a contest called a fire muster. Raj and I have directions for a fire muster you can try at home. Thanks for coming to visit all of your friends at the Main Street Fire Station.

Firefighters are always busy. They check their fire trucks, engines, cars, and ambulances twice a day. Firefighters practice their skills and learn how to use new equipment. They also visit schools. Firefighters are always happy to teach others how to stay safe.

RAJ AND TIM'S FIRE MUSTER

A fire muster is a contest in which fire companies show off their skills. They race up fire-truck ladders. They try to shoot the longest streams of water. They see who is fastest at hauling water the old-fashioned way, with bucket brigades. Being quick is an important skill for firefighters.

Give this muster a try:

1. You see flames coming out of a neighbor's window. What number would you call?

2. You leaned too close to a lit candle. Your shirt is on fire! Practice STOP, DROP, AND ROLL:

    STOP where you are!

    DROP to the ground!

    ROLL around, over and over, to put out the fire!

3. Hold a fire drill with your family. This kind of drill is called E.D.I.T.H. (Exit Drills in the Home). Choose a safe place to meet, then practice getting out of your house—fast! Use a watch or stopwatch to time yourselves. How long did it take for everyone to get to the meeting spot? Try the drill again and see if you can do it even faster.

4. Practice different kinds of drills. Pretend it's dark and you can't see. Wear a blindfold over your eyes and crawl from different parts of your house to the nearest door, feeling your way. Pretend there's a fire right outside your bedroom door. Stuff a blanket or towel under the door. Then crawl to your window and wait for a firefighter.

5. Be a smoke-detector detective. How many smoke detectors does your house have? Is there one outside each bedroom? Is there one on each level of your house? Ask a grown-up to test the batteries in each detector. Even if the batteries are okay, they should be replaced every six months. Mark the dates on a calendar to help you remember. Smoke detectors save lives.

All finished?

You are now a member of Raj and Tim's Firefighter Safety Team.

FUN FACTS

- Sometimes firefighters work during the day. Other times they work at night. Then, they sleep at the firehouse.

- In the 1700s, some towns passed fire safety laws. Every home had to keep a fire bucket near the front door. There were no fire trucks or hoses, so people formed bucket brigades. Bucket brigades worked like this: People stood in two long lines. The people in one line passed buckets of water. The person at the end of that line threw the water on the fire or nearby buildings. The other line of people passed the empty buckets back to be refilled. Everyone had to help.

- The first fire muster was held on July 4, 1849, in Bath, Maine.

- Many new fire stations don't have fire poles. Some firefighters got hurt sliding down the poles as they rushed to fires, so the stations put in slides.

- The "Jaws of Life" is a special rescue tool. Firefighters use it to remove people from crushed vehicles.

- Fire Prevention Week is held every year around October 9. The date reminds us of the Great Chicago Fire in October of 1871.

WORDS TO KNOW

arson—the crime of setting fire to a building or property on purpose

company—a group of firefighters who work together

dispatcher—someone who takes emergency phone or radio calls and alerts the firefighters

fire engine—a vehicle used by firefighters to carry hoses, pull in water from a hydrant, and pump it back out through smaller hoses

fire muster—a competition to judge the quickest, strongest, and best fire-fighting teams and individuals

hazardous—dangerous

hydrant—a large, upright pipe with a valve that draws water from the city's water supply. Hydrants supply water for fighting fires.

ladder truck—a truck used by firefighters to reach tops of buildings. The ladder is part of the truck.

turnout gear—the special clothing and equipment firefighters wear to fires

TO LEARN MORE

At the Library

Bourgeois, Paulette. *Fire Fighters*. Toronto: Kids Can Press, 2000.

Demarest, Chris L. *Firefighters A to Z*. New York: Margaret K. McElderry Books, 2000.

Hayward, Linda. *A Day in a Life of a Firefighter*. New York: Dorling Kindersley Pub., 2001.

Raatma, Lucia. *Fire Fighters*. Minneapolis: Compass Point Books, 2000.

On the Web

Meet Smokey the Bear

http://www.smokeybear.com

For games, stories, and activities related to fire prevention.

New York City Fire Department

http://www.nyc.gov/html/fdny/html/home2.html

For safety tips and information about New York City firefighters.

Want to learn more about fire stations? Visit FACT HOUND at *http://www.facthound.com*.

INDEX